W9-AGZ-580

The Tower of London

Author: Colin Hynson

WORLD ALMANAC® LIBRARY

Please visit our web site at: www.worldalmanaclibrary.com
For a free color catalog describing World Almanac® Library's list
of high-quality books and multimedia programs, call 1-800-848-2928 (USA)
or 1-800-387-3178 (Canada). World Almanac® Library's fax: (414) 332-3567.

Library of Congress Cataloging-in-Publication Data

Hynson, Colin.
    The Tower of London / by Colin Hynson.
      p. cm. — (Places in history)
    Includes index.
    ISBN 0-8368-5813-1 (lib. bdg.)
    ISBN 0-8368-5820-4 (softcover)
    1. Tower of London (London, England)—Juvenile literature. 2. London (England)—Buildings,
structures, etc.—Juvenile literature. 3. Great Britain—History—Juvenile literature. I. Title. II. Series.
DA687.T7H96   2005
942.1'5—dc22   2004056928

First published in 2005 by
World Almanac® Library
330 West Olive Street, Suite 100
Milwaukee, WI 53212 USA

This U.S. edition copyright © 2005 by World Almanac® Library. Original edition copyright © 2004
ticktock Entertainment Ltd. First published in Great Britain in 2004 by ticktock Media Ltd.,
Unit 2, Orchard Business Centre, North Farm Road, Tunbridge Wells, Kent, TN2 3XF.

Consultant: John Rogers

Photo credits: Alamy: 33; Art Archive: 7R, 10L, 11R, 27L, 27R, 30L, 31R; Bridgeman Art Library: 6L, 16L,
20T, 26, 28L, 29R, 32L, 32R, 40L; Corbis: 18TR, 24BL, 39L, 42, 43B, 44L, 44–5, 45R; Heritage Images: 4BL,
14R; Historic Royal Palace: 9, 20B, 21T, 23B, 24–5, 35, 36, 38L, 39R, 43T; London Aerial Photo Library: 18–19

Printed in the United States of America

1 2 3 4 5 6 7 8 9 09 08 07 06 05

Contents

Introduction   4–5

Chapter 1: **How It Was Built**   6–9

Chapter 2: **The Tower through History**   10–17

Chapter 3: **Exploring the Tower**   18–25

Chapter 4: **The People**   26–33

Chapter 5: **Tower Traditions**   34–35

Chapter 6: **Uncovering the Past**   36–39

Chapter 7: **A Day in the Life**   40–43

Chapter 8: **Preserving the Past**   44–45

Glossary   46–47

Index   48

The Tower of London is one of the most famous buildings in the world. Initially founded in 1066 as a mighty fortress to protect a new foreign king, it has served many purposes in its long history. The Tower has served as a royal residence, an armory, home of the Royal Mint, a formidable and occasionally brutal prison and site of executions—and, today, a dazzling tourist attraction.

A Paranoid King?

King Edward the Confessor's death, in January 1066, sparked a series of events that would change the course of English history. On his deathbed, the king was persuaded to pass the throne to his brother-in-law, Harold, Earl of Wessex. However, Harold had already promised Duke William of

This map from 1588 shows the Tower of London as it looked at that time, situated on the Thames River.

Normandy that he would let him become king. A furious William ordered his troops to invade England, and Harold was killed at the Battle of Hastings in 1066. William was crowned king at Westminster Abbey on Christmas Day. The new king was faced with the daunting task of controlling a largely hostile population of more than two

million with an army of just 10,000 knights. To protect himself from attack, William began a castle-building program across the country. A wooden castle was erected but was soon pulled down to make way for the new stone building that later became known as the White Tower.

Tower Expansion

For the next 250 years, the Tower continued to grow at an impressive rate. By the early 14th century, the basic layout of the Tower that survives today had been achieved by the construction of two towered curtain walls and a moat. Henry III (1207–1272) and Edward I (1272–1307) were the monarchs who had the greatest impact

The Battle of Hastings of 1066 is illustrated in detail in the Bayeux Tapestry. This scene from this famous tapestry shows King Harold being killed.

on the Tower's development. Until the 16th century, the Tower of London was the principal royal home. It was also the home of the Office of Armory, the Royal Mint, the crown jewels, and the monarch's personal zoo. But the Tower is perhaps best remembered as a prison and site of criminal executions. Famous prisoners held at the Tower included Henry VIII's second wife, Anne Boleyn; Sir Walter Raleigh; Nazi war criminal Rudolf Hess; and the Kray twins, the notorious London gangsters. Today, the Tower of London is one of the most famous tourist attractions in the world. Millions of people visit this sprawling monument every year to see its many treasures for themselves.

The Tower of London as it appears today. The vast complex of buildings has come a long way since the White Tower was built under the orders of William the Conqueror in the late 11th century.

Soon after William was crowned king of England on Christmas Day in 1066, work began on the White Tower, the original Tower of London. The location for this new castle was chosen to take advantage of one of the strongest parts of the city wall left behind by the Romans. It also had the Thames River flowing beside it, which added another line of defense.

Prime Location

The choice of position for the Tower of London was not a difficult decision for William and his military advisors. The Roman city of Londinium had been surrounded by 3 miles (5 kilometers) of stone walls of up to 20 feet (6 meters) in height. One of the strongest and most important parts of this wall was on a small hill overlooking the Thames River in the southeastern corner of the city. This was obviously the best place for William to build his main castle in London. He could use part of the Roman wall to strengthen the castle. This location would also make the castle the first building seen by any ship sailing up the Thames.

Materials

The original castle was completed quickly. Like nearly all of the castles built by William, it was

This illustration from a 13th-century French manuscript shows how laborers transported blocks of stone up ramps for building.

made of wood and earth. William knew, however, that this could only be a temporary structure. He needed a more permanent castle made of stone. Not only would this be stronger and easier to defend, but by using stone, it sent the message that William and the Normans were in England for good. In 1067, the

wooden structure was pulled down so that a new, stronger castle could be built in its place. The King chose the Bishop of Rochester, Gundulf, well-known for designing churches and castles in France, to be the architect. Although little is known about when work on the Tower began and finished, building was well advanced by the time of William's death in 1087. The fact that the Tower's first prisoner came to the Tower in 1100 suggests that the building must have been completed by that time.

Building a castle of timber and earth was quick and easy and did not require a great deal of skill or labor. However, building a stone castle like the White Tower took many years. If nothing was available locally, building material had to be brought in and both skilled and unskilled labor organized. All of this was organized by the king's officials alongside skilled builders known as master masons. Other skilled workers, such as blacksmiths and carpenters, had to be brought in, as well. The unskilled work was done by gangs of local Anglo-Saxons who were probably not paid for their labor.

Building the Tower

The first job that had to be done was to see if the ground could support such a large building. Since it was so close to the Thames, the ground was very soft. Therefore, before the White Tower was built, trenches up to 15 feet (4.5 meters) deep were dug and filled with rubble. This provided the support for a plinth on which the tower would be built. As the walls of the tower began to rise, it became necessary to put up scaffolding. As the Tower was built higher, long poles were placed in special holes that were built into the walls. These poles were then tied together with rope. These holes, known as putlog holes, can still be seen in the White Tower and in many other Norman castles.

Medieval masons are shown building a wall in this German manuscript from 1068.

The types of stone chosen as the materials from which to build the White Tower were a brown limestone known as Kentish Ragstone, from Kent, England, and a cream-colored limestone from Caen, France. The stone would have been cut to the right size and shape at the quarry before being transported by boat to the building site. One of the great advantages of having a large river next to where the castle was being built was that it made transporting such heavy materials a less grueling and time-consuming task. The mortar, a mixture of sand and lime used to cement the stones together, was probably made on the tower's site.

Huge vats in which the mortar was mixed would have been built by the river. It could then be taken by wheelbarrow to the builders. Many of the tools used to build the Tower of London would not have been all that different from those used on modern building sites.

These modern-day masonry tools are similar to the tools that were probably used to build the Tower of London.

The Tower of London

Medieval pictures of castles and cathedrals being built show that wheelbarrows, plumb lines, chisels, and drills were used. Human-powered cranes were used to raise stones to the heights at which they were needed.

Changing Castles

The earliest castles in England were built in the "motte-and-bailey" style. This kind of castle includes a fortified wooden structure situated on a mound of earth in which the lord or king lived. This structure was surrounded by a defense wall which led down the hill and enclosed the castle buildings at the foot of the hill. The initial reason for the emergence of these castles was to offer some kind of defense to villagers who were being terrorized by raiders. However, these wooden castles soon proved inadequate, being vulnerable to fire and weather damage, and were replaced by stone castles. Various different styles of stone castle were built thereafter, trying different shapes and building materials with the goal of increasing security. The late 13th century saw the rise of the "concentric castle," which featured an interior dwelling for the royalty or nobility that was protected by many rings of walls, with the inner walls being higher than the outer ones. The Tower of

In the early Medieval period, the "motte-and-bailey" castle (above) was the common style in Europe. The castle itself was made of wood and built on a mound (or motte) while the rest of the castle buildings were built on flat land. When William I became king, he recognized that a wooden castle was not going to be secure enough. His fortress was added to over time to become a concentric castle like the example shown below.

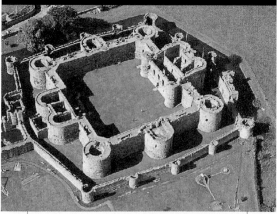

London that visitors see today has grown and changed in many ways since the White Tower was completed. These changes reflect the emergence of improved architectural styles and methods of fortification.

Early Expansion

The first king to make major changes to the Tower was Richard I (1189–1199). When he left England to take part in the Crusades, he left his chancellor, William Longchamp, in charge of the kingdom. Longchamp began a building program at the Tower of London, and by the end of the 12th century, the area of the Tower had doubled. This was done by digging new ditches and building new walls, with a new tower (the Bell Tower) at the southwest corner. In the 1220s, the boy king Henry III began a major expansion of the Tower. He improved the kitchen and great hall and built two towers next to the river— the Wakefield Tower and the Lanthorn Tower. Then, in the 1230s, Henry had a new wall containing nine towers built at the east, west, north, and southeast sides of the Tower. Between 1275 and 1285, Edward I created a new wall outside the existing wall and a bigger moat. He also built the Beauchamp and St. Thomas Towers. The first two Tudor monarchs also made many changes to the Tower.

Medieval Renaissance

During the 19th century, a number of changes were made to the Tower. The Waterloo Barracks were put up to accommodate a thousand soldiers and several towers were restored, renovated, or rebuilt. During this period, it was popular to return buildings to their original styles. In 1852, the Beauchamp Tower was restored with a Medieval appearance. Similarly, the Salt Tower, the White Tower, St. Thomas' Tower, and the Bloody Tower were all renovated, while the Lanthorn Tower was rebuilt. Much of what appear to be original in these parts of the Tower of London are actually Victorian-era "improvements."

This reconstruction of the Tower of London shows how it would have looked in 1200. The additions by Richard I and William Longchamp—chiefly, the addition of new sections of curtain wall and the massive Bell Tower in the foreground—are clearly visible

Tales & Customs — A Restless Queen

Some people claim to have seen the ghost of Anne Boleyn (Henry VIII's second wife) at the Tower. Alleged sightings of her ghost outnumber sightings of others. According to eyewitness accounts, she normally appears as a headless figure near the Queen's House. She has been identified by the period and style of her clothes, and she has also been seen heading a procession of nobles in the Chapel of St. Peter ad Vincula.

CHAPTER 2

The Tower Through History

The Tower was not primarily intended to be a castle that protected the people of London from attack. Neither was it supposed to be the principal place where the kings and queens of England would live—although many monarchs did in fact occasionally live there. It was initially built to provide a symbol of royal power and to serve as an easily defendable place for the royal family to take shelter during periods of unrest.

The First Siege

The first known attack on the Tower took place in 1191, during the reign of Richard I. King Richard spent many years away from his kingdom fighting in the Third Crusade. During this time, he left England in the hands of his chancellor, William Longchamp, who ordered a massive expansion of the Tower. Richard's younger brother Prince John saw Longchamp as a barrier to his taking the English throne for himself. He therefore laid siege to the Tower in order to get rid of Longchamp. The new defenses held up against this attack, but Longchamp had to surrender when food in the Tower ran out.

Wat Tyler, the leader of the Peasants' Revolt of 1381, was eventually apprehended and killed, as illustrated here.

Noble Rebellion

When King John died in 1216, his nine-year-old son Henry III, took the throne. At the time, much of the country was ruled over by nobles who had rebelled against King John. The Tower was actually controlled by an ally of the rebellious nobles, Prince Louis of France. It was not until 1217 that Henry III drove Louis out so that he could take control of his country and his most important castle. Twice in the 1230s, Henry had to face rebellions by England's nobles. Both times he retreated to the Tower for safety. It was as a result of relying on the Tower that he began a massive expansion of the Tower's defenses in the 1230s. Edward III was the last English king to begin a major building

Time Line

1066	William, Duke of Normandy, becomes King of England.		1238	King Henry III's expansion of the Tower begins.
1067	Wooden castle built on the site of the Tower.		1241	White Tower is whitewashed.
c.1078	Work on the White Tower begins.		1275	King Edward I continues with improvements to the Tower.
1101	The Tower's first prisoner, Ranulf Flambard, escapes.			
1191	First known attack on the Tower.		1381	Peasants' Revolt forces King Richard II to take shelter in the Tower.

program at the Tower. His father, Edward II, was forced by Parliament to give up the throne in 1327, and his 17-year-old son, Edward III, took the throne.

His reign was peaceful, and he made some improvements to the Tower's defenses, including rebuilding parts of the Bloody Tower.

PEASANTS' REVOLT

The Peasants' Revolt of 1381 was one of the largest rebellions in English history. The revolt was caused by the introduction of a hugely unpopular type of poll tax. King Richard II and his family took shelter in the Tower while up to 20,000 rebels ransacked London. The rebels actually took control of the Tower for a short while, killed several of the King's closest advisors, and looted his apartments. The revolt ended when the King promised to meet the people's demands. However, he never had any intention of keeping his promises.

In 1483, the 12-year-old rightful heir to the throne, Edward V, and his younger brother were imprisoned in the Tower of London. They disappeared shortly afterward and were never seen again.

The Wars of the Roses, which occurred between 1455 and 1485, were the result of two rival noble families fighting for the throne.

Wars of the Roses

The Medieval period came to a close after a long series of civil wars between 1455–1485, known as the Wars of the Roses. The Wars of the Roses were fought between the noble families of Lancaster and York, both of whom claimed the throne. The Tower again played a key role during this period. Two kings were both killed there in mysterious circumstances during the Wars of the Roses—Henry VI in 1471 and Edward V in 1483. The civil wars came to an end with the death of Richard III in 1485 and the arrival of the first Tudor king, Henry VII. At that time, the Tower became less a place of royal protection and more a prison for those who opposed the monarch.

1445	Wars of the Roses.
1465	King Edward IV holds lavish courts at the Tower.
1471	King Henry VI is murdered at the Tower.
1483	"The Princes in the Tower" disappear.

Henry VIII created the Protestant Church of England when he broke from the Roman Catholic Church in the 1530s.

Religious Rifts

Both Henry VII and Henry VIII made improvements to the Tower. However, the main improvements made by both were more aesthetic than practical. They focused on making the royal lodgings more comfortable rather than improving the Tower's defenses. This shows how confident the first Tudor kings were that they would not have to face the same kind of rebellions endured by the medieval monarchs. In the 1530s, Henry VIII began to pull the English Catholic Church away from the control of the pope in Rome and to create a new Protestant Church. This break was caused by Henry wanting to divorce his first wife, Catherine of Aragon, because she did not bear him a son, so that he could marry Anne Boleyn. The pope refused to give his permission for the divorce to go ahead. This division caused religious conflict in England and the Tower was used by Tudor monarchs as a place to deal with those who opposed them. Henry VIII made several such people prisoners in the Tower.

Unjust Executions

In 1535, two of Henry VIII's most important advisers—Sir Thomas More and the Bishop of

Queen Elizabeth I, daughter of Henry VIII, also ordered many important Catholic figures to be imprisoned in the Tower.

Rochester—were executed for refusing to accept Henry as the new head of the English Church. In May 1536, Henry used the Tower to imprison and execute his second wife, Anne Boleyn. In 1542, Catherine Howard, Henry's fifth wife, was also executed in the Tower. Before the Catholic Mary I, Henry VIII's

Time Line

1528	The last year the Tower is used as a royal residence.
1535	Sir Thomas More is executed.
1536	Anne Boleyn is executed at the Tower.
1554	Execution of Lady Jane Grey takes place at the Tower.
1554	Princess, later Queen, Elizabeth is imprisoned in the Tower.
1601	Execution of Robert Devereux, Earl of Essex, at the Tower.
1605	The Gunpowder Plot is thwarted.
1618	Sir Walter Raleigh is executed at Westminster.

oldest daughter, came to the throne in 1553, she had to deal with an attempt to put Henry's Protestant great-niece, Lady Jane Grey, on the throne. Jane was executed at the Tower in 1554. Mary then brought the English Church back under Catholic control. Like her father before her, she met resistance, and the Tower was used to imprison those who defied her.

Resistance to the Monarch

Unlike her half-sister, Mary, and her father, Henry VIII, Elizabeth I was reluctant to execute her political and religious enemies. She preferred to rule with the support of as many of her subjects as she could get. However, that did not stop her from using the Tower as a place to imprison those who resisted her rule, and executions were ordered when she saw it as necessary. In 1601, just two years before her death, Robert Devereux, the Earl of Essex, was imprisoned and beheaded at the command of Elizabeth after he led a rebellion against her. Elizabeth died childless, and the English throne was passed to the Scottish king, James. During his reign, the relationship between the monarch and Parliament began to worsen. After James's son, Charles I, inherited the throne, that relationship eventually broke down into civil war by 1642. In 1643, Parliament took control of the Tower to help defend London. The civil war ended in 1649 when Charles I was executed. England became a republic controlled by Oliver Cromwell. Cromwell was the first ruler of England to place soldiers in the Tower on a permanent basis.

Henry VIII used the Tower of London as a place of imprisonment and execution for anyone who dared to oppose him. Two of his six wives were sentenced to live their final days in the Tower before they were executed.

The Tower of London

Charles II placed cannons in front of the Tower facing the Thames River. It was clear he would not hesitate to retaliate against an attack from any source, including his own people.

the Grand Storehouse, erected in 1688. The Tower was used to store weapons until the start of World War I in 1914. Also during the reign of Charles II, the crown jewels were first put on display to the visiting public. The jewels were moved to a new site in what is now called the Martin Tower.

Coins were produced at the Tower's Royal Mint until the early 19th century. The Royal Mint is now located in Wales.

A Message of Military Might

In 1660, two years after the death of Oliver Cromwell in 1658, Charles I's son (also named Charles) returned from exile and assumed the throne of England and Scotland. Like Cromwell, Charles II believed that the Tower was the key to controlling London. It was under Charles II that cannons were first placed on the walls facing both the Thames River and the city itself. The message to the people of London was clear. If necessary, the Tower would be used by the king against his rebellious subjects. Several new buildings were put up inside the Tower to store munitions and to provide workshops. The largest building was

Time Line

1674	Skeletons of two boys are discovered and are believed to be those of the "Two Princes."
1780	Last executions on Tower Hill.
1810	The Royal Mint is removed from the Tower.
1820s	The Tower is no longer used as a regular prison.
1826	The Duke of Wellington becomes Constable of the Tower.
1834	The royal menagerie is removed from the Tower.
1840s	Emergence of the Chartist movement.

Animals and Money

The Tower was, for several centuries, the home of the royal menagerie. While it may well have been King John who first introduced exotic animals to the Tower, it was his son, Henry III, who really developed the Tower Menagerie. Henry III owned an elephant, leopards, and a polar bear. By the 1500s, the animals in the menagerie had become an important tourist attraction. James I was fond of watching animal fights and came to the Tower to view different animals fighting each other. In the early 1830s, William IV moved the animals out of the Tower to the new London Zoo.

The Tower was originally the site of the Royal Mint, where coins were first made during the reign of Edward I. Originally, blocks of gold and silver were cut into discs and stamped with the royal insignia. Machinery was introduced to the Mint under Charles II, making it possible for coins to be produced much faster. By the end of the 1700s, it was clear that there was not enough space at the Tower for the Mint. A new Mint outside the Tower began operating in 1810.

Victorian Times

In the 1840s, the Chartist movement shook London. The Chartists were calling for major political reform, including extending the vote to all adult men. England's rulers were nervous about the Chartists and decided to make the Tower an easier place to defend. Between 1848 and 1852, new gun emplacements and a northern bastion were added to strengthen the Tower against attack.

Throughout history and up to the present day, official ceremonies have taken place at the Tower of London. In this picture, taken in 2001, a new constable of the Tower of London is installed.

The Tower of London

This 19th-century painting depicts the fire of 1841 that razed the Grand Storehouse completely to the ground. Queen Victoria's husband, Prince Albert, ordered for the Waterloo Barracks to be built in its place.

the end of Queen Victoria's reign in 1901, half a million people were visiting the Tower each year.

Wartime Prisoners

In the 20th century, England fought in two world wars, and the Tower of London once again became a place to imprison and execute enemies of the state. At the beginning of World War I (1914–1918), eleven German spies were imprisoned in the Tower and later executed by firing squad inside the Tower. Unlike many other parts of

Prince Albert, shown in this 19th-century painting, was responsible for a great proportion of the changes to the Tower during Queen Victoria's reign.

In 1841, a fire swept through the Grand Storehouse at the Tower of London. The Waterloo Barracks were built on the site of the Grand Storehouse. The Barracks were built to house 1,000 soldiers. When the Chartist threat had died down, the country appeared to be at peace again, and the Tower took on a different role. Although sightseers were first admitted in 1660, the last part of the Victorian period saw a huge increase in visitors to the Tower. In 1841, the first official guidebook to the Tower was published and ten years later a specially built ticket office was erected. By

Time Line

Year	Event	Year	Event
1841	The Grand Storehouse is destroyed by a fire.	1852	Beauchamp Tower is restored.
1841	The first official guidebook to the Tower is published.	1870	The crown jewels are moved to Wakefield Tower.
1843	Queen Victoria orders the moat to be drained.	1914	Eleven German spies are executed at the Tower.
1845	The Waterloo Barracks are built.	1939	The tower is closed to the public and the crown jewels are removed.
1850s	The Tower was heavily restored in the 1850s.		

Nazi leader Rudolf Hess flew from Germany to Scotland in an attempt to call a truce with the Allies during World War II.

London, the Tower did not suffer from any bomb damage during World War I, although one bomb landed harmlessly in the moat. The Tower suffered much more bomb damage during World War II. The bastion built on the northern wall to defend the Tower against the Chartists was hit, along with some other 19th-century buildings. During World War II, the Tower was closed to the public and the crown jewels were taken to a secret location. Everyone was encouraged to grow their own food, and even the moat of the Tower was used for growing food.

World War II saw the last execution at the Tower when a German spy named Josef Jakobs was shot in 1941. The chair that he sat in when he faced the firing squad was put on public display for many years. During World War II, the Tower became most famous as the prison of Rudolf Hess. Hess was very close to Adolf Hitler and was a very important member of the German government. In 1941, he flew a plane to Scotland in a desperate attempt to negotiate peace between Britain and Germany. The British government refused and placed Hess under arrest inside the Tower. He was held at the Tower for four days, after which he was sent to Nuremberg, in Germany, for trial and placed in prison (see also p. 33).

Postwar Peace

At the end of the war, the Tower of London returned to its peaceful role as a top tourist destination. In 1952, however, the Tower briefly became a prison once more for some high-profile prisoners. This would be one of the last times the Tower was used for this purpose. The infamous gangsters known as the Kray twins were called up to start their National Service in the army. When they failed to show up, they were arrested by the police and taken to the Waterloo Barracks, where they were held overnight. The Kray twins then spent the next two years either on the run from the army or in military prison.

1941   German deputy Rudolf Hess is temporarily imprisoned in the Tower after attempting to fly from Germany to Scotland—allegedly to negotiate an end to World War II.

1946   The tower is reopened to the public.

1948   The crown jewels are returned to the Tower.

The function of the Tower of London has changed greatly over the centuries of its existence. Each of its buildings has a unique function and legendary status. In spite of the fact that the tower and all of its components have stood for nearly 1,000 years and will continue to stand for years to come, the Tower was not primarily intended to act as London's primary symbol of military might. Read the following pages for a closer look—inside and out!

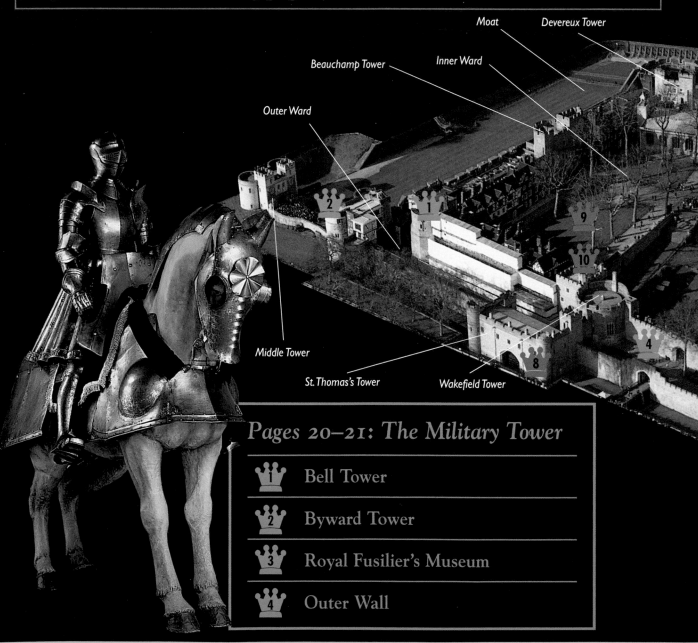

Moat · Devereux Tower · Beauchamp Tower · Inner Ward · Outer Ward · Middle Tower · St. Thomas's Tower · Wakefield Tower

Pages 20–21: The Military Tower

- **Bell Tower**
- **Byward Tower**
- **Royal Fusilier's Museum**
- **Outer Wall**

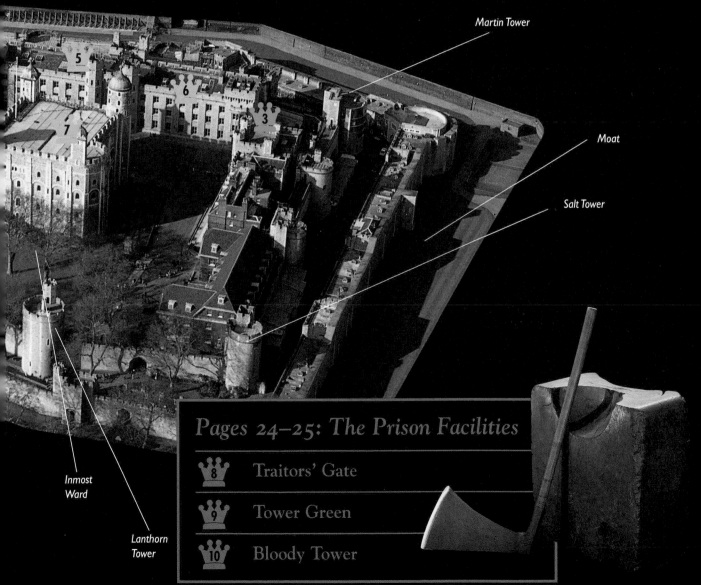

Pages 22–23: Waterloo Barracks and the White Tower

 5 Waterloo Barracks

 6 The Crown Jewels

 7 White Tower

Martin Tower

Moat

Salt Tower

Inmost Ward

Lanthorn Tower

Pages 24–25: The Prison Facilities

8 Traitors' Gate

9 Tower Green

10 Bloody Tower

👑 Bell Tower

The Bell Tower is situated at the southwest corner of the Inner Ward. Built in the 13th century, the Bell Tower earned its name from having a belfry at the top. Historically, the bell was rung as an alarm, but today it is only rung to advise visitors when closing time is approaching.

Legend says Elizabeth I walked along this path on top of the outer wall between the Bell Tower and the Beauchamp Tower when she was a prisoner at the Tower.

👑 Byward Tower

It is possible to enter the Tower by passing through the Middle Tower and then crossing a drawbridge to the Byward Tower. The Byward Tower originally had two portcullises (huge wooden grills that could be raised or lowered). If you look up as you pass through the archway you will see a series of "murder holes." Legend states that defenders of the Tower could use these holes to pour boiling oil on attackers. They were more likely, however, to have been used to douse fires.

The twin-towered gatehouse known as the Byward Tower was built during the reign of Edward I.

The Tower of London houses two collections of military artifacts. The first is in the White Tower. The second is housed in the Royal Fusilier's Museum (above), which was established in 1685.

 ### Royal Fusiliers' Museum

On the east side of the fortress is a 19th century building that houses the Royal Fusiliers' Museum. The Royal Regiment of Fusiliers was founded in 1685 by James II (1685–1688) in order to protect the royal guns inside the Tower. The Regiment has been involved in many military campaigns including the American Revolution, the Boer War, both World War I and World War II, and the 1991 Gulf War. Memorabilia from these campaigns is on display in this museum.

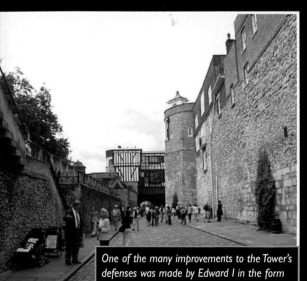

One of the many improvements to the Tower's defenses was made by Edward I in the form of an additional outer wall (left).

 ### Outer Wall

When visitors walk into the Tower, they will see that it is defended by two walls. Some of the inner wall was built by William Longchamp, Chancellor to Richard I (1189–1199). Between 1275 and 1285, Edward I added an entirely new Outer Wall in order to make the Tower of London into a near-impregnable fortress. Invaders could not get in and royal prisoners could not get out.

The Waterloo Barracks were built in 1845, and they replaced the Grand Storehouse which was destroyed by a fire in 1841. The cannons in front of the building were captured from the French at the Battle of Waterloo.

Waterloo Barracks

The Waterloo Barracks were built in the 19th century while the Duke of Wellington was constable of the Tower. The Barracks were intended to accommodate about 1,000 soldiers. They were designed in the neogothic style, which ref___ how much people in the 19th century admired medieval styles. The building was named after the Battle of Waterloo, in which the British were part of the coalition that defeated Napoleon Bonaparte in 1815.

The Crown Jewels

Today, the Waterloo Barracks is the home of the crown jewels. The crown jewels have been on display to the public since the 17th century. They have been in different parts of the Tower since the 14th century, except during World War II when they were moved to a secret location.

The crown jewels are currently located in Jewel House in the Waterloo Barracks.

White Tower

The building with the strongest royal connection and the earliest existing structure in the Tower of London is the White Tower. It took about thirty years to build and was completed by 1100 during the reign of William II. It is called the White Tower because it was whitewashed when Henry III was king. Its main entrance is through a door on the ground floor.

The oldest building of the Tower of London, the White Tower gained its name when Henry III had it whitewashed in the 13th century.

Displayed throughout the White Tower are pieces from the Royal Armories collection. The collection includes weapons for the armed forces from the medieval period right up until the start of World War I. This collection of weapons dates from the reign of Henry VIII right up until recent times. Notable pieces in the collection are the armor of Henry VIII and Edward I. The Spanish Armory contains the Tower's torture instruments.

The Chapel of St. John the Evangelist in the White Tower was where the Royal family and court worshiped. It was built during the Norman period.

On the first floor are rooms that were used by kings and queens for entertaining and for important royal events. One room that was used for many such occasions is the **Chapel of St. John the Evangelist**. The body of the wife of Henry VII lay in this room after her death. Henry VIII's daughter, Mary I, married King Philip of Spain in this room in 1554, even though Philip was not actually present at the time of the wedding. It was used as a chapel in medieval times, but from the 16th to the 19th centuries, it was used to store state records.

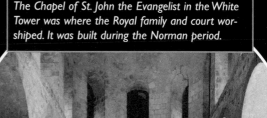

The entrance to St Thomas's Tower inherited the name "Traitors' Gate" because many alleged traitors were brought to prison by a boat that entered through it.

8 Traitors' Gate

The watergate entrance to the Tower has been known as "Traitors' Gate" since the 17th century. Although originally built so that the king or queen would have an easier access route to the Tower, the gate gained its name because of the number of prisoners accused of treason who were brought into the Tower via this entrance. The gate is located beneath St Thomas's Tower. It was built by Edward I in the 13th century.

9 Tower Green

The main open area of the Tower of London is known as Tower Green. Tower Green was a private open space for about three hundred years. Before this, Tower Green was the site of seven private executions in the 15th and 16th centuries. Private executions were reserved for the most important prisoners. Among the prisoners whose lives ended there were Anne Boleyn, Catherine Howard, and Lady Jane Grey. Today, a plaque stands in the place where the scaffold stood, recognizing the lives that ended there.

The open area behind the Bloody Tower is known as Tower Green. Seven executions took place on Tower Green during the 15th and 16th centuries.

Built in the 13th century, the Bloody Tower is a part of the Tower of London that was used as a prison. It was believed that the "Princes in the Tower" were murdered in this tower, and it is because of this it was given its grizzly name. The reality is, however, that the princes probably were not held in it.

👑 The Bloody Tower

Before St. Thomas's Tower was built, there was another tower that sat on the edge of the Thames River and served as the gateway between the river and the Tower of London. This tower is now known as the Bloody Tower. Some of the stories and legends that emerged from the Tower of London were supposed to have taken place in the Bloody Tower. The Bloody Tower was first built in the 1220s. A new floor was added in about 1360, during the reign of Edward III.

Parts of the Bloody Tower are decorated to represent different historical periods, and these displays are often updated. This bed (above) is a replica of the one slept in by Sir Walter Raleigh when he was a prisoner in the Tower.

The Bloody Tower was designed to provide a comfortable environment, with a fireplace, tiled floor, and large windows. It was usually set aside as a guest room for anybody visiting the constable of the Tower. It also served as a place to keep some of the more important prisoners, such as Sir Walter Raleigh, who spent thirteen years in these lodgings.

CHAPTER 4

The People

The Tower of London has always been linked with the English, and, later, the British, monarchy. The monarchs saw the Tower as a symbol of their strength and prestige. They used the Tower not only to control the often-rebellious population of London and to imprison their political and religious enemies, but also as a place of retreat in times of strife and even as a place of entertainment. Nearly every king and queen has left some kind of mark on the history of the Tower. Some even ordered famous historical figures to be imprisoned and executed in the Tower.

William the Conqueror

The monarch who started building the Tower of London was William I, also known as William the Conqueror. He built the original Tower after he had taken the crown by force. His victory in 1066 at the Battle of Hastings led to England having a new royal family, a new style of building, a new language, and a new set of rulers. He was a brilliant and ruthless military leader. He managed to hold on to his lands despite rebellions from within and invasions from the outside. One such invasion was led by the king of France. When William invaded England, he had planned to keep many of the English nobles in their places. However, continuing resistance to his taking the English crown meant that he replaced the English nobles with reliable French-speaking nobles. He also built castles and cathedrals across the country to help maintain control over his new subjects. There are many monuments to

This detail from the 11th-century work called the "Bayeux Tapestry" shows soldiers heading off to join King Harold in the Battle of Hastings.

Tales & Customs — Ghost at the Gate

One of the earliest reported ghost sightings at the Tower was of St. Thomas à Becket. It was said that when work on Traitors' Gate was nearly finished in 1240, a violent storm caused the gate to collapse. After the exact same thing happened a year later, a priest claimed to have seen the ghost of Sir Thomas à Becket striking the walls with a crucifix. The priest said that the ghost was proclaiming that the new building was not for the common good but "for the injury and prejudice of the Londoners, my brethren."

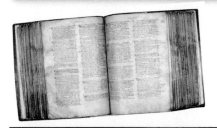

The Domesday Book was an account of all property owned in England in 1085. It has proved an invaluable resource for learning about people in the Middle Ages.

William's harsh rule in British towns and cities. However, William I was also responsible for one of the most remarkable documents ever created in English history. At the end of 1085,

William ordered that a record be made of all of the land and property in England. Agents were sent around the country and their findings were compiled in the Domesday Book.

Merciless Edward

Another medieval monarch that had a great impact on the Tower was Edward I, who reigned from 1272 to 1307. No other monarch made such an effort to rule the whole of Britain. He conquered Wales and built a series of castles to defend his new kingdom. He also invaded Scotland on several occasions and managed to influence who was placed on the Scottish throne. The improvements that he made to the Tower were purely to make sure that he could keep control of his capital. Edward I is also known as the

This illustration from a 13th century French manuscript shows Edward I seated on his throne before his subjects.

monarch who expelled the Jews from England.

Royal Executions

The most tragic members of the royal family to have a link with the Tower were the so-called "Princes in the Tower." When King Edward IV (1461–1470 and 1471–1483) died, his two sons,

This 16th-century painting by Holbein captures the beauty of Anne Boleyn, second wife of Henry VIII. She was imprisoned for allegedly committing adultery and beheaded on Tower Green in 1536.

princes. The bones were transferred and buried in Westminster Abbey. In 1933, the marble urn in which the bones were placed was opened up for inspection. An examination of the bones concluded that they were the skeletons of two boys of the same ages as the two princes were when they disappeared.

A Kingdom Divided

In Tudor times, the larger-than-life figure of Henry VIII (1509–1547) brought the Tower of London into yet another major part in the history of England. Beginning in the 1520s, Henry was becoming increasingly worried that he did not have a son to take the throne when he died. He only had a daughter, Mary. He blamed his wife, Catherine of Aragon, for this and decided to marry Anne Boleyn instead. The pope, however, did not allow the king to divorce Catherine. Henry reacted by breaking the English Church from the Roman Catholic Church and setting himself up as the head of the Church in England. Under the new church, Henry could divorce and marry again. Many objected to Henry's divorce and

refused to acknowledge him as head of the Church. Henry reacted by having Sir Thomas More and the Bishop of Rochester arrested and placed in the Tower of London. They were both executed in 1535.

Lady Jane Grey was executed in 1554.

Edward and Richard, were taken to the Tower by their uncle, Richard (the deceased king's brother). Twelve-year-old Edward was supposed to have become Edward V, but he was never crowned. Instead, his uncle was crowned Richard III in 1483—and the two princes mysteriously disappeared. There were rumors that Richard had ordered their murder—rumors that Richard made no attempt to deny. In 1674, two skeletons were discovered in the Tower. The size of the bones suggests that they could have been those of the two

Tales & Customs — Lives Cut Short

The spirits of the two "Princes in the Tower" were occasionally reported seen in the Bloody Tower, where they were believed to have been imprisoned. They were said to be wearing white nightgowns and holding hands. If an observer dared approach, however, they were said to shrink into the wall and disappear. Yeoman warders have reported hearing the sound of a child crying in buildings called the Casemates, which are around the outer walls of the Tower. Those who heard the sound always investigated but found nothing.

Innocent Women

Henry VIII's second wife, Anne Boleyn, also met an unhappy end in the Tower. She had married Henry in 1533. In the same year, she gave birth to Elizabeth. Again, Henry began to look for someone who would produce a son, and he chose Jane Seymour. Anne was arrested on trumped-up charges in 1536 and taken to the Tower, where she was eventually executed. Catherine Howard, Henry VIII's fifth wife, also met her end at the Tower.

One of the saddest royal demises that took place at the Tower was that of Lady Jane Grey. By the time Edward VI died in 1553, England had completed its break with the Roman Catholic Church and had become a Protestant country. The new

This 19th-century painting shows the two princes who mysteriously disappeared in the Tower. It is widely believed they were murdered.

monarch was the Catholic Mary I. She was determined to return the English Church to the arms of Rome. Protestant nobles conspired to put Lady Jane Grey, the great-niece of Henry VIII, on the throne. For nearly two weeks they appeared to be successful. A series of uprisings, however, propelled Mary onto the throne. Lady Jane Grey, who was never more than a pawn in a game, was subsequently arrested and placed in the Tower. She was executed there in February 1554.

The Tower of London

A Comfortable Prison?

The Tower of London has been used as a prison for most of its history. Many of the prisoners were not jailed for any crimes that they actually committed but because they had some-how earned the displeasure of the reigning monarch. The Tower gained the reputation as a grim and foreboding prison. For many prisoners, however, prison life inside the Tower could be quite comfortable—as long as they had enough money to pay for it. The first recorded prisoner in the Tower was Ranulf Flambard, the Bishop of Durham. He was put in the Tower in 1100 by Henry I after he was accused of extortion. Flambard lived in some style in the White Tower. He had his own servants and had many visitors from the outside world. On February 2, 1101, he threw a party for his guards. He allowed the guards to drink as much wine as they wanted. That evening, as the guards were deep in a drunken sleep, he lowered a rope out the window, climbed down to the ground, and made his getaway. That not only made him the first known prisoner of

Sir Thomas More was the lord chancellor when Henry VIII wanted to divorce his first wife, Catherine, so he could marry Anne Boleyn. More resigned from his post and was subsequently imprisoned and executed outside the Tower on Tower Hill.

the Tower but also the first to make an escape.

An Unlucky Escape Attempt

Besides the members of the English royal family who were imprisoned in the Tower, certain non-English royalty also spent time there as prisoners. The Welsh prince Gruffydd ap Llewelyn was imprisoned by Henry III. In 1244, Gruffydd tried to escape from the Tower on a rope. Sadly, the rope broke and he fell to his death. It was written that when he was found, "his head and neck were driven into his breast, between the shoulder."

High Profile Prisoners

The most notable foreign prince who was imprisoned in the Tower was Charles, Duke of Orleans. He was captured at the Battle of Agincourt in 1415. In those days, prisoners were often held for money. They would be freed after a ransom was paid.

Charles was a prisoner in England for twenty-five years before his ransom was eventually paid. It was rumored that during his long days in the Tower,

Since 1078, the Tower of London has seen hundreds of prisoners The details of each has been recorded in The Book of Prisoners.

Tales & Customs — Strange Scents

Several visitors and staff have reported smelling something strange in the Chapel of St. John in the White Tower. The smell was described as a strong, perfumelike incense, and is was said to be strongest at night. Strangest of all, in 1817, the keeper of the crown jewels, Edmund Swifte, and his wife said they saw a strange cylinder filled with a white and blue liquid move around the room and then slowly fade into the wall as they were were having supper with their family in the Martin Tower.

Charles turned to writing poetry. After Charles's release, it was said that Henry VII had the Duke's poetry bound into a book that Henry presented to his bride, Elizabeth of York. The book also contained several painted pictures, or illuminations.

Under the Tudor kings and queens, many prisoners ended up in the Tower because they did not agree with the religious practices of their monarch. Under Henry VIII, Edward VI, Mary I, and Elizabeth I, the Tower became a prison and place of death for many well-known religious figures. One of the most famous of these was Sir Thomas More. More was a well-known scholar and writer. He opposed both Henry VIII's decision to divorce his first wife and his decision to break with

This illumination from the Duke of Orleans's book of poems shows him as a prisoner in the Tower. It is one of the earliest images of the Tower of London.

the Roman Catholic Church. In 1529, More became lord chancellor, but he resigned in 1532 when he felt that he could no longer support Henry VIII's policies. He tried to live a quiet life after that, but Henry saw him as a threat and had him imprisoned.

After refusing to accept Henry as the new head of the English church, he was executed on Tower Hill in 1535.

The Tower of London

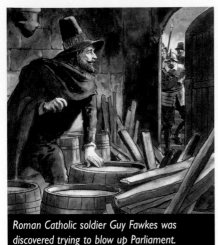

Roman Catholic soldier Guy Fawkes was discovered trying to blow up Parliament. He was taken to the Tower and later executed.

Caught Red-Handed

Guy Fawkes was another famous prisoner placed in the Tower. In November 1605, a group led by Robert Catesby thought they could end the persecution of Roman Catholics in England by blowing up James I and members of the House of Lords and House of Commons. The plot was uncovered, and Guy Fawkes was discovered on November 5 under the parliament buildings with a large amount of gunpowder. He was immediately taken to the Tower as a prisoner. The warders at the Tower needed a confession from Fawkes as well as more information about his fellow conspirators. On November 16, Fawkes signed his confession. His barely legible signature suggests that he was in an incredible amount of pain after being tortured into signing a confession.

In England, the failure of the Gunpowder Plot is celebrated every year on November 5 with the lighting of fireworks.

An Adventurer Confined

One of England's best-known sailors and explorers was Sir Walter Raleigh. He ended his days as a dis-

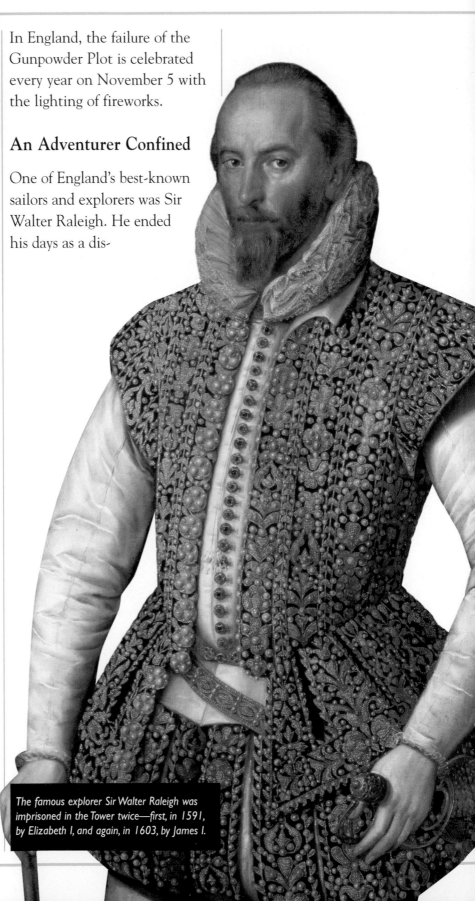

The famous explorer Sir Walter Raleigh was imprisoned in the Tower twice—first, in 1591, by Elizabeth I, and again, in 1603, by James I.

graced prisoner in the Tower. In the 1580s, Raleigh took part in a series of adventures and fought for Elizabeth I in Ireland between 1580 and 1581. During this time, he became one of the queen's favorites. In 1591, it was discovered that Raleigh was secretly married to one of the queen's ladies-in-waiting. Elizabeth flew into a jealous rage and had Raleigh thrown into the Tower. He was released after five weeks when he promised to share any treasure he captured from his expeditions. These expeditions often led to clashes with Spanish ships. Elizabeth I did not mind this too much, particularly after the failed Spanish Armada in 1588. The new king, James I, was eager to make peace with the Spanish, and he had Raleigh imprisoned in the Tower for a second time in 1603, this time for allegedly conspiring against

Rudolf Hess (right) was one of the highest-ranking members of Hitler's (left) Nazi Party. In 1941, Hess flew an airplane from Germany to Scotland. No one knows for sure his reason for doing this, but many believe he wanted to call a truce with the Allies. Instead, he was captured and imprisoned in the Tower.

James I and trying to place the king's cousin, Lady Arabella Stuart, on the throne. Raleigh remained a prisoner at the Tower until 1616. During this time, he conducted scientific experiments and wrote the first volume of his ambitious *History of the World*.

His second child, Carew, was even baptized at St. Peter ad Vincula in 1605. Raleigh was eventually executed in 1618 at Westminster, after leading an unsuccessful expedition to find the legendary city of El Dorado, during which he clashed again with the Spanish.

Modern-Day Prison

The Tower of London was used continually as a prison until the 1820s. Just over one hundred years later it was again used as a temporary prison for the Nazi war criminal Rudolf Hess. Hess was third-in-command to Adolf Hitler, the leader of Nazi Germany. Hess was taken prisoner and temporarily put in the Tower. In 1945, Hess was tried for war crimes at Nuremberg, in Germany, and he was sentenced to life in prison. He died in 1987 at the age of 92 (see p. 17).

Tales & Customs — The Roaming Raleigh

Alleged sightings of the ghost of Sir Walter Raleigh are among most commonly reported ghost sightings at the Tower. Many people believe that, because of Raleigh's long period of incarceration in the Tower and the amount of freedom given to him to walk around, he may be coming back to visit old acquaintances. Several yeomen claim to have seen Raleigh near the guardroom. He is said to appear in a very solid form and to remain only for short periods of time.

CHAPTER 5

Tower Traditions

> ***L**ike many other famous buildings, the Tower of London has many customs and traditions. They range from the striking uniforms worn by the yeoman warders to the keeping of ravens that nest adjacent to the Wakefield Tower.*

It is not known exactly when ravens first came to the Tower. The birds are cared for by the ravenmaster who raises them from the time they are babies.

Watching Over the Tower

One of the best-known sights at the Tower are the yeoman warders. They are often called "beefeaters," although the warders never use this name for themselves. Historically, their job was to guard royal prisoners and the Tower gates. Their red-and-gold uniforms are only worn on special occasions, such as church parades or when an important visitor comes to the Tower. They usually wear a red-and-blue uniform (*pictured right*) that was introduced in 1858. Now that the prisoners are gone, the main duties of the yeoman warders are to look after the many tourists who visit the Tower. They are still, officially, bodyguards for the monarch. All yeoman warders must be former members of the armed forces with at least twenty-two years service. The Tower of London is also watched over by about thirty ravens. The birds are tended by one yeoman master called the ravenmaster.

Ceremony of the Keys

One of the most important ceremonies that the yeoman warders take part in happens every night when the Tower is closed. This is the Ceremony of the Keys, in which the Tower is locked and made secure. It has happened every night for hundreds of years. This probably makes it the oldest military ceremony in the world. Nobody knows

Yeoman warders have protected the Tower for hundreds of years. Today, their duties are very different from hundreds of years ago because there are no longer any prisoners to guard.

when the ceremony started but it probably dates back to when the White Tower was built by William the Conqueror. The Ceremony of the Keys starts every night at 9:50 P.M. The chief yeoman warder, accompanied by an armed guard, carries a lantern with a candle burning inside as he walks around the Tower. He uses the Queen's keys to lock up all the gates on the outer walls before marching to the Bloody Tower, where the keys are handed over to the Resident Governor for safekeeping.

St. Peter ad Vincula is one site of the Beating of the Bounds, a ceremony that takes place every three years on Ascension Day at parishes around the country.

Other Ceremonies

Another important ceremony that takes place at the Tower is the Ceremony of Lilies and Roses. In 1471, Henry VI was supposedly murdered in the Oratory at Wakefield Tower. Every year on the anniversary of his death, school pupils from Eton and King's College place lilies and roses on the spot where he was killed. Henry VI had helped to found both the school and college. The "Beating of the Bounds" ceremony takes place every three years on Ascension Day, which is forty days after Easter. The earliest record of the Tower taking part in this custom dates back to at least 1381. The ceremony takes place outside the Tower. Thirty-one boundary stones that mark the Tower's boundary are beaten by local choirboys with long sticks, or "willow wands." It is believed that, originally, during the Beating of the Bounds, children were beaten so that they would remember the borders of their parish.

Tales & Customs — The Ravens

Nobody knows when the ravens first appeared in the Tower, but they were soon protected by a legend that arose around them. Some people believed that without them the Tower and the entire country would fall. One of Charles II's astronomers complained that the ravens were interfering with his observations. The King ordered them to be killed. However, when he found out about the legend, he allowed a small number to remain. Their wings were clipped to make sure they did not fly away.

Very little is known about the early history of the Tower. There are plenty of documents relating to the building of the Tower in the medieval period, but most of these are only accounts of the money spent on the construction, rather than information about building methods and cultural practices. What actually happened in the Tower in the first few centuries of its existence is also difficult to piece together, largely because there are few written records. The number of literate people during the Tudor period was far less than today.

This Iron-Age skeleton was excavated from a site near Lanthorn Tower (one of the Towers that faces the Thames River) in 1976.

What Excavations Yielded

Many gaps in the knowledge of historians have been filled by archaeological findings. There have been many archaeological digs in and around the Tower. Excavations in the 1960s and 1970s revealed much about the early history of the Tower and also about what happened on its site before the arrival of the Normans. In 1976, a skeleton was discovered during an excavation close to the Lanthorn Tower. The skeleton was from the Iron Age—just before the arrival of the Romans in A.D. 43. Archaeologists believe that the skeleton belonged to a man who was buried before the Romans began to settle in what would eventually become the city of London.

Early Castles

When the Normans began their castle-building program in England, they erected motte-and-bailey castles. These were wooden structures consisting of a defensive wall surrounding a large building on top of a mound. The Tower of London, however, was different. The Romans had built 3 miles (5 km) of stone walls around London. One of the largest and strongest parts of this wall was where the Tower of London was eventually built. Since it had the Thames River on one side and the Roman wall on another, all William I had to do was dig a ditch on the other sides. The buildings inside were then safe.

In the time leading up to Halloween 2001, a team of ghost hunters spent several nights in the Tower of London. These experts used temperature gauges, infrared light, and "black cameras" that can see in the dark. All of this equipment was trained on four of the Tower's allegedly haunted locations: Sir Walter Raleigh's study in the Bloody Tower; the Bell Tower; the Chapel of St. Peter ad Vincula; and the Beauchamp Tower. A live Web cast allowed people around the world to watch for ghostly apparitions. Nothing was seen or recorded during this time.

Uncovering the Evidence

Nobody knew exactly where these ditches were. This was important to learn because it would tell historians how much space the first Tower of London actually took up. These ditches were eventually discovered during archaeological excavations in the 1960s. The foundations of Roman buildings

Evidence from archaeological digs has taught us a great deal about the Tower of London.

have also been discovered both close to and underneath the White Tower.

Ancient Trees

One of the ways that archaeologists can date a building is through the science of dendrochronology. This science examines the timber used in a building to determine its age. As a tree grows upward and outward, it leaves a ring in its trunk. Each ring represents one year's growth. There is still some debate about when work on the White Tower actually began. However, applying dendrochronology to the timber in the White Tower shows that building was certainly under way by 1081.

Reflooding the Moat

One of the most important discoveries about the Tower of London occurred between 1995

The number of rings represents the tree's age. This tree is eleven years old.

The center ring indicates the earliest year of the tree's life.

Dendrochronology is the science of examining the rings in a tree trunk in order to determine the age of a tree.

and 1997. For much of the Tower's history, its moat was filled with water from the nearby Thames River.

The moat was drained and filled in during 1843 after it had gained a reputation as a smelly and unhygienic place. In 1995, a project called the Tower Environs Scheme was launched.

Excavations, such as this one that took place in the moat outside the Develin Tower in 1997, have revealed many previously unknown facts about the Tower's history.

Trees with History

When they dug in the western moat, near Beauchamp Tower, archaeologists discovered the remains of a high-quality building. It was known that Henry III had built an entrance to the Tower, but until 1995, nobody was sure of its exact location. Wooden piles around the building remains were found, which supported documentary evidence that a Tower building fell down in the mid-13th century. Dendrochronology dated the wood in these piles to the winter of 1240 and 1241.

Tower Mills

The presence of mills at the Tower is known through a document from 1276. This document mentions how 600 trees had been felled and brought to the

In 1956, this workman found two pieces of 18th-century pottery during maintenance work near the Wakefield Tower.

The idea of this project was to improve the appearance of the area around the Tower; to improve access for visitors; and to reflood the moat. Before proceeding, however, it was important to ensure that nothing of historical importance would be lost in the process. Therefore, excavations needed to take place. As a consequence, the moat was not reflooded, and it remains empty today.

Tales & Customs — Special Salutes

Ever since the invention of guns, they have been fired in celebration as well as in war. Firing in celebration is known as a "salute." The Tower of London had one of the earliest salutes in England, when guns were fired to celebrate the coronation of Anne Boleyn in 1533. Today, the guns are fired to signal the birthdays of the Queen of England and her husband, Prince Philip. They are also fired on the anniversary of the Queen's coming to the throne and at the State Opening of Parliament.

The finding of this 15th-century fish trap with the remains of a fish inside of it proved that fishing once took place in the Tower's moat.

Tower to provide the piles on which the mills would sit. It was not known exactly where these mills were built. In 1996, archaeologists discovered a large number of tree trunks that were proved to have been cut down in 1276—the year that the mills were built.

A Historic Fishing Spot

One of the most interesting artifacts found in the moat was a 15th-century wicker fish trap. The trap was found lying in its original position, with stones inside it to weigh it down and wooden pegs to secure it to the bottom. It only had been suspected that fishing took place in the moat. This trap was evidence that it had.

An average day in the life of the Tower of London has, in many ways, remained the same over hundreds of years. And, yet, at the same time, each day is unique. The day starts officially when the Tower gates are unlocked at six o'clock in the morning. Yeoman warders, or beefeaters, are required to stand guard inside the Tower. Besides their daytime duties, every yeoman warder is obliged to be on duty one night each month.

The Tower hosts many exhibitions about the Tower's role through history. This 1840s advertisement features the Tower of London in the background.

A Top Tourist Spot

For tourists, the Tower does not officially open until 9 A.M. (except on Sundays and Mondays, when it opens at 10 A.M.). There are many things at the Tower for visitors to see and do. The yeoman warders are stationed around the Tower. They have been trained to answer questions and act as guides for the many tourists.

Living History

The Tower of London holds many exhibitions that concentrate on particular aspects of its history. There are also regular "living history" events that usually take place during school holidays and on weekends. These events involve guides dressing up in historical costumes and using parts of the Tower as a stage to tell stories. There are also costumed events in which signifi-

This painting shows a yeoman warder taking a group of Victorian children on a tour of the Tower of London. Tourists have been permitted to visit the Tower since the 16th-century.

cant events that took place at the Tower, such as the siege of the Tower of London in 1471 and sword fights, are re-created. Christmas is also an interesting occasion at the Tower, during which historical festivities are the theme. There are also interactive events at the Tower during which, for example, visitors can help "prisoners" escape or vote on what happened to the two vanished princes. The Tower is a very popular destination for schoolchildren. About 12,000 children visit the Tower each year.

Going Off with a Bang

Guns are brought into the Tower especially to conduct salutes on important dates throughout the year. Each year, these dates include the anniversary of the English monarch's coronation, the English monarch's birthday, and the State Opening of Parliament. Salutes are also given to acknowledge visits by foreign heads-of-state. The tradition of gun salutes at the Tower was established in about the 1530s.

A Unique Workforce

The day-to-day running of the Tower is handled by a resident governor. In the past, this job was done by the Constable, the monarch's representative at the Tower. The post of constable still exists, but it mostly has a ceremonial role these days. A new constable is appointed every five years. The installation ceremony takes place on Tower Green. The Lord Chamberlain, who represents the monarch, hands the new constable the keys to the Tower.

Every five years, an installation ceremony involves the ceremonial handing over of keys to the new Constable of the Tower.

The Constable then hands the keys to the Queen's House to the Resident Governor, giving him permission to live there. There are about 180 people working inside the walls of the Tower. They range from workers in souvenir shops and restaurants to maintenance and cleaning crews to marketing and public relations people. Unusual positions at the Tower include the ravenmaster, who looks after the Tower's ravens, and the crown jeweller, who comes to the Tower in the January of each year to clean the crown jewels.

An Unusual Home

Since the Tower was first built, there have been people living there. Today, many of the people who work in the Tower of London also call it home. About thirty-five yeoman warders live in the Tower with their families. Their neat-looking townhouses face onto Tower Green. Other

The Tower is locked at the end of each day by the Chief Yeoman Warder, who is accompanied by a military guard, in a historic tradition known as the Ceremony of the Keys.

Tales & Customs — In the Drink

On February 18, 1478, the Duke of Clarence allegedly drowned in a barrel of Malmsey wine at the Tower of London. The obvious reason for his drowning in a barrel of wine might appear to be that he fell in while drunk, but this wasn't the case. Instead, it is likely that he was executed on the orders of his brother, King Edward IV, for alleged involvement in several major conspiracies against the King. The Duke's unusual death has been immortalized by Shakespeare in his play Richard III.

officials such as the Governor, Deputy Governor, and the Chief Exhibitor of the Crown Jewels also live inside the walls of the Tower of London.

Most of the residents of the Tower live in the Casemates, which are buildings set into the walls of the Tower. The Resident Governor lives in the Queen's House on Tower Green. The Tower of London also has a resident chaplain.

The chaplain holds services at St. Peter ad Vincula, the

The Captain of the Guards is the most senior of all the yeoman warders. He is also known as the Chief Yeoman Warder.

chapel within the Tower. There are regular Sunday services as well as special services. The chaplain also takes part in special occasions such as the Beating of the Bounds. Members of the public are welcome to any of these services.

Behind the Scenes

The Tower of London is usually closed to the public at 5 P.M. in the winter and at 6 P.M. during the rest of the year. The Tower is then locked up with the ancient Ceremony of the Keys. Afterward, the yeoman warders can relax in their own private club, which is the oldest club in London. The Victorian-style interior of the club is decorated with regimental heraldry on the walls, along with original newspaper and magazine cartoons with military themes, especially

those that relate to the Tower. The club also contains plaques presented to the yeoman warders from military and police organizations from all over the world.

One of the main roles of yeoman warders today is to act as guides to visiting tour parties.

CHAPTER 8

Preserving the Past

The Tower of London is one of the most important buildings in British history and a very important part of the London tourist industry. More than two million people visit it every year. This means that looking after the buildings and interiors of the Tower of London is incredibly important. This care and maintenance is handled by an organization called Historic Royal Palaces.

Natural Threats

The Tower faces several threats from the environment. Changes in air temperature can cause damage to the masonry on the outside of buildings. This is known as "thermal movement." Water is also a problem. Many of the stones and bricks used in the buildings within the Tower are porous. This means that a little bit of water can seep into them. This water can damage both the surface and inside of the stone. Inside the buildings, light can cause damage to walls and furniture. Organic materials like wood, fabric, and paint can fade if they are exposed to light. Insects and beetles, such as the Death-Watch beetle, can also cause damage to wood.

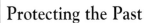

The Crown Jeweller cleans the crown jewels once a year. In this photo, he is cleaning the beautiful Imperial State Crown.

Car Pollution

The Tower is situated next to a busy road in the center of London. The vibrations from the heavy vehicles that pass by has an effect on the structure of the Tower. Exhaust fumes not only make dust, which coats the Tower (making it harder to clean), but also contribute to making rain slightly acidic.

Protecting the Past

The outside of the Tower sometimes needs to be cleaned regularly to prevent damage to the stone and bricks. Ordinary cleaning systems can destroy the historic fabric of a building, so specialized techniques are used. Structural engineers also monitor the condition of the buildings and must decide whether they

Tales & Customs — Lost Love and Lost Lives

The interior walls of the Beauchamp Tower are covered in inscriptions left by the prisoners kept there in the years when the Tower was still a prison. On the walls of one of the state prison rooms are the letters, "JANE, JANE." These letters are alleged to have been carved by Lord Guildford Dudley during his imprisonment and separation from his wife, Lady Jane Grey, who was at the same time a prisoner elsewhere in the Tower. Both were executed at the Tower in 1554 (see p. 29).

need reinforcing. Inside, the conservation team tests light levels, temperatures, humidity and ventilation, and also monitors dust levels. Delicate items such as textiles and paintings need specialized care. Historic Royal Palaces has a laboratory that provides scientific advice on conservation issues—testing the strength of materials, checking light- and heat-aging, and dust monitoring. Damage to historic paintings and materials is also monitored and conservation repairs are carried out when necessary.

Replacing the Past

The conservation staff have guidelines that they follow when it comes to repairing or replacing things. If possible, historic material should not be removed. All

Reconstructions, like these that took place at the Royal Chamber of the Wakefield Tower, need to be conducted very carefully. All materials must be checked before use to ensure nothing will be damaged in the process.

Replacing stained-glass windows at the Tower can be a painstaking process. Many people work to ensure that the end result is in keeping with the style of the building.

new work should use the right material for the job and all repairs and replacements should be reversible, so that the impact on the Tower is minimal.

Glossary

Anglo-Saxons: inhabitants of England (of Germanic descent) from the 5th century A.D. through to the Norman Conquest in 1066.

armory: a place in which arms and ammunition are stored.

barracks: buildings or sets of buildings designed as accommodations for soldiers.

bastion: a projecting part of the wall of a castle that makes it possible to defend the wall of the castle on either side.

beefeater: another term for a yeoman warder; a security guard at the tower of London.

campaign: series of military operations with a particular aim or purpose.

chapel: a usually small place of worship associated with an institution that can be set aside for private use or for a small group.

Chartists: a group of reformers in 19th-century England who made demands for political and social improvements.

civil war: a war or a conflict fought between two groups within the same country. The war between King Charles I and Parliament under Oliver Cromwell was a civil war.

concentric: having a common center. The Tower of London is called a concentric castle because its interior is protected by many circles of walls.

constable: a title normally given to the governor of a royal castle who acts on behalf of the king or queen. It is also the name for any important officer in a royal household.

Crusades: the series of military campaigns attempted by Christian powers to regain ownership of the Holy Lands from the Muslims.

defenses: means, methods, or structures for protecting something from attack, often consisting of physical walls, towers, soldiers and weapons.

dendrochronology: a method of determining the age of a piece of wood by examining its rings.

Domesday Book: an official record of all the land and property owned in England in 1086.

excavations: cavities formed by digging or scooping, especially those made during archaeological investigations.

execution: killing of a person who has been legally condemned to death.

exile: a person who has been barred from living in his or her native country.

extortion: the act of obtaining by force, threat, or unfair means.

fortification: something put in place to defend or strengthen against attack.

fortress: a building or town that has been strengthened against attack.

garrison: an army of troops stationed in a particular town to defend it from attack.

illuminations: illustrations that decorate the pages of medieval manuscripts.

keep: the strongest part of a castle, designed to defend the rest of the castle complex.

Londinium: the ancient Roman name for the city of London.

loops: narrow, vertical slits in a wall that can be used by soldiers inside to defend a building.

menagerie: an early type of zoo in which captured wild animals were put on display.

mint: a place where coins are made, usually officially set up by a government and often operating under tight security.

moat: a wide ditch filled with water that surrounds and protects a castle or town.

monarch: a ruler of a country such as a king or queen.

mortar: a mixture of lime, cement, and water that is used for holding bricks in place.

motte-and-bailey: an early type of castle favored by the Normans when they first invaded England. The motte was a wooden fortress built on top of a mound of Earth. The bailey is an outer wall that surrounds the mound and has other buildings inside it. Most castles of this type were replaced by stone castles.

munitions: military weapons, ammunition, and equipment.

noble: a man or woman who belongs to a high-ranking social class, often by birth; also known as an aristocrat.

oratory: a place of prayer, especially a small private chapel.

ordnance: weapons, ammunition, and military supplies; also the part of an army responsible for taking care of the weapons, ammunition, and other supplies.

persecution: the practice of treating people in a cruel or harsh way, especially over a long period of time.

portcullis: a strong and heavy gate that can be lowered or raised, usually meant to protect the entrance to a fortress.

ransacked: thoroughly searched and often damaged for the purpose of robbery or plunder.

rebellion: opposition to authority resulting in uprising against existing rule; also known as revolt.

regiment: a permanent army unit.

salute: the firing of guns or cannons in order to pay homage or show respect.

scaffold: a raised wooden platform on which prisoners were executed. The platform would be built so that the execution could be seen better by the people who had come to watch it.

siege: a military operation in which an army tries to force the surrender of a town or castle. Sieges usually involve either attacking a town or castle directly or surrounding it and waiting for its inhabitants to run out of necessities such as food.

traitor: a person who has acted in a way that hurts or damages his or her own country or monarch.

treason: the crime of betraying one's country.

Tudor: the royal dynasty that held the English throne from the time of Henry VII (1485) until the death of Elizabeth I (1601).

whitewash: a mixture of lime and water used for painting walls white.

yeoman warder: a member of the team of security guards responsible for the Tower of London; also known informally as a "beefeater."

Index

A

Albert, Prince 16
Arundel Castle 4–5

B

Beating of the Bounds 35, 43
Beauchamp Tower 8, 9, 16, 38, 45
"beefeaters" *see* yeomen warders
Bell Tower 8, 20
Bloody Tower 9, 11, 25, 29
Boleyn, Anne 5, 9, 12, 24, 28, 29, 38
bomb damage 17
Byward Tower 20

C

cannons *see* guns
Casemates 29, 42
castles 4, 5, 7, 8, 36
Catesby, Robert 32
Catherine of Aragon 12, 28
Ceremony of the Keys 10, 34–35, 42, 43
Ceremony of Lilies and Roses 35
Chapel of St. John the Evangelist 23, 43
Chapel of St. Peter ad Vincula 9, 33, 35, 43
Charles, Duke of Orleans 30–31
Charles I 13
Charles II 14, 15
Chartists 15, 16
Church 12, 28, 29, 31
Civil War 13
Clarence, Lionel, Duke of 42
Constable of the Tower 25, 41
Cromwell, Oliver 14, 27
crown jewels 5, 14, 16, 17, 22, 42, 44
Crusades 10

D

dendrochronology 37, 38, 39
Develin Tower 38
Devereux, Robert, Earl of Essex 12, 13
Domesday Book 27
Dudley, Lord Guildford 45

E

Edward the Confessor 4
Edward I 10, 11, 15, 20, 21, 24, 27
Edward II 11
Edward III 11, 25
Edward IV 11, 28
Edward V 11, 28
Edward VI 29, 31
Elizabeth I 12, 13, 20, 24, 29, 31, 33
Elizabeth of York 31

escapes 30
excavations 36, 37, 38-39
executions 12, 13, 24, 25, 27-30
exhibitions 40

F

Fawkes, Guy 32
fish trap 39
Flambard, Ranulf, Bishop of Durham 10, 30
fortification 8

G

ghosts 9, 27, 29, 33
Grand Storehouse 14, 16, 22
Grey, Lady Jane 12-13, 24, 28, 29, 30, 45
Gruffydd ap Llewelyn 30
guidebooks 16
Gundulf 6
Gunpowder Plot 12, 32
guns 14, 15, 21, 38
    see also salutes

H

Harold, Earl of Wessex 4
Hastings, Battle of 4, 26
Henry I 30
Henry III 8, 9, 10, 14, 17, 22, 27, 38
Henry VI 11, 35
Henry VII 11, 12, 23, 31
Henry VIII 12, 28, 29, 31, 32
Hess, Rudolf 5, 17, 33
Historic Royal Palaces 44
Howard, Catherine 12, 24, 29

I

Jakobs, Corporal Josef 17
James I 13, 15
James II 21
Jewel House 38
Jews 27
John, King 10

K

keys 10, 34–35, 41, 42, 43
Kray twins 5, 17

L

Lanthorn Tower 8, 36
"living history" 40
Londinium 6
London Zoo 15
Longchamp, William 8, 9, 10, 11, 21
Louis, Prince of France 10

M

Martin Tower 14
Mary I 12, 13, 23, 28, 29, 30, 31
masons and tools 6-7
menagerie 14–15
Middle Tower 20
mills 39
moat 16, 37–38
More, Sir Thomas 12, 24, 29, 30, 31–32

O

Office of Armory 4, 5
Outer Wall 21

P

Parliament 13
Peasants' Revolt 11
Poll Tax 11
Princes in the Tower 11, 14, 25, 28, 29
prison 4, 5, 12, 30, 33

Q

Queen's House 9, 41, 43

R

Raleigh, Sir Walter 5, 12, 25, 32–33
ravenmaster 35, 41–42
ravens 34, 35, 42
Richard I 8, 9, 10, 21
Richard II 11
Richard III 11, 28, 42
Richard, Prince 28
Rochester, John Fisher, Bishop of 12, 29
Romans 6, 36
Royal Armories 23
Royal Fusiliers' Museum 21
Royal Mint 4, 5, 14, 15

S

St. Martin's Tower 5
St. Thomas's Tower 8, 9, 24, 25, 43
Salt Tower 9
salutes 38, 41
Scaffold Site 24
Seymour, Jane 29
Spanish Armada 33

T

Thames, River 4, 6
Thomas à Becket, St. 27
Throne Room 23
tourists 4, 5, 16, 17, 40
Tower Environs Scheme 38

Tower Green 13, 24, 43
Tower Hill 14
Tower of London
    building 4–8
    conservation 44–45
    damaged by fire 16
    illustrations 2–3, 4, 9, 15, 16, 18–19, 31
    royal residence 4, 5, 11, 12, 14
    siege (1191) 10
Tower Wharf 40
Traitors' Gate 24, 27, 37

V

Victoria, Queen 16

W

Wakefield Tower 5, 8, 16, 35, 45
Wars of the Roses 11
Waterloo Barracks 9, 16, 17, 22
Wellington, Arthur Wellesley, Duke of 14, 22
White Tower 5, 6–7, 8, 9, 10, 22, 37
William I (the Conqueror) 4, 5, 6, 8, 10, 26-27
William II 22
William IV 15
World War I 14, 16-17
World War II 17, 35

Y

yeoman warders 29, 33, 34, 35, 40-41, 42, 43
Yeoman Warders' Club 43